Cripple Poetics:
A Love Story

Petra Kuppers & Neil Marcus

photographs by
Lisa Steichmann

Homofactus Press
Ypsilanti, Michigan

Published in 2008
by Homofactus Press, L..L.C.
www.homofactuspress.com

Copyright © 2008 by Petra Kuppers and Neil Marcus.
Photographs Copyright © 2008 by Lisa Steichmann

Printed in the United States of America

ISBN: 978—0—9785973—3—7

1. Poetry. 2. People with Disabilities and the Performing Arts. 3.
People with Disabilities and Literature. 3. Sexuality—Literature.
4. Self in Literature. 5. Literature and Photography. I: Kuppers,
Petra II: Marcus, Neil III: Lisa Steichmann.

cover design: Jeremy Weichsel
http://www.flickr.com/photos/jeremywww/

Cripple Poetics: A Love Story

One: In Pursuit of a Kiss
Seeds
Landscape
Disability Culture
Biology
Two: Cripple Poetics
Three: Echoes

For all the lovers in the world,
for the human movement:
let's dance
for Lydia
for Spalding Gray,
with thanks to disabled people
everywhere.
Thanks to our friends.

Acknowledgements:

Huron River Review: "Night Ice"
Breath and Shadow: "Crip Music"
The New Sun: "Disabled Country"
Disability Studies Quarterly: various
Dogzplot: various
About Performance: "Zydeco Egg"
Contemporary Theatre Review: "West Coast Contact
Improv"
Slow Dancing to Invisible Music, a chapbook by Inglis
House: "The Question of Cripple"
Wordgathering: "At the Gynecologist's"

One: In Pursuit of a Kiss

Kuppers and Marcus

The Metaphor of Wind in Cripple Poetics

How can I speak of cripple and not mention the wind.
How can I speak of crippled and not mention the heart.
Heart, wind, song, flower, space, time, love. To leave
these absent is to leave cripple in stark terms.
As if we were made of medical parts and not flesh and
bone.

There is always wind in my cripple
Off shore breezes.
Scented nightflowering vines.
Wild salsa dances that run past midnight

Cripple is not extraordinary or ordinary.
Cripple is a full plate
A blown about newspaper
An ox in a rice field, ploughing earth

Alchemy

                              When
              you are fully in the softness   flow
          of the flesh   open grail: now
                                     hold blood in a warm
      remember earth   remember water

    and touch the tremor in the scar's heaving life.   mouth
When you embrace with all your   dragon
  might this last   fall into

    bejeweled branch   laugh

    remember air   remember fire
    feel the breath   go
    whistle between your ache of   ready to let
        teeth.   you are
                          When

Seeds

Wanted: Someone to share warm summer nites in their coolness and cold winter nites in their warmth. Yes. I'm a handsome romantic 53 yr old spastic revolutionary with a vision. Lets have dinner. I live a poetic life. I wish intimacy and to share a life with beauty art love community

Are you excited adventurous about life. Lets meet.

Wanted: Creative, artistic, personal partner and love, for ample woman with ample imagination, performances under her belt, songs in her mouth, traveling wind in her hair, limping through life. Crip culture card carrying members preferred. Searching for cuddlebug, floordancer, tri-lingual romantic jester for a poetic life. Gender: open. Size: no issue. I like them strong and large. Has to be able to keep up, relax down, size up, seize me.

Weve been awaiting this moment for so long.
We meet at last. hello my dear. I am petra.
On meeting, we sit on the floor to dance.
Dancing hands is how we dance today. Dancing souls.
Dance in revolution. Dance in love.

There is a lot of shadow play in this performance
A lot of old voices revisiting the present.
I find myself moving close to petra.
Wanting to be close and not alone.

I found myself stroking her bare leg under her pants in
a dance lecture she invited me to participate in.
"touching History" we danced together. In front of
class.
Despite, im sure i was playing appropriately cool
though. a bit aloof.
Admiring the academician who dances and speaks
poetry.

she asked, "how does our touch in this dance inform
you ?
what information is communicated in this way ? "

four months later im in Michigan Petra and I are rolling
round on the floor
In front of a curtain.behind a curtain.under a sheet of
red silk

" how does our touch in this dance inform you ?
what information is communicated in this way ? "

In a moment of hiding from the cameras spotlight, I
stole a kiss under the covers.
Petra months later tells me this was the moment I stole
her heart.
Was this the moment our relationship began, she asks.
Did it start in Berkeley when we first met ?
I thought you were a Lothario.

I of course, a man, deny everything. Uuuuuhhhhhhh.
"no, I didn't notice attraction."
No, I had no inkling.
I had no idea.

I am becoming conscious.

Swimming
    in
    a
         figure
            eight.

It was dark in the room. I remember his touch: very smooth hand, very warm skin. I remember an embrace, and him holding me. We've never met before, but we sank down onto the floor together, moving our arms together, wondering at each other.

           Kelp
       flow

          Otter
             pelt. S   ilver wire
                                    coat.

                           Jelly
                     fish: co
             lored puff-ball
         ball   et

       Rainbow light
    effect
      in
       in
visible creatures;

the inference
of watching

keep seeing lots of seeds from trees here..millions in
the streets they look like miniature chinese dumpling
wraps the size of the little fingernail.to me loneliness
magnifies pain

sending a hug. neil
i enjoy being around people who are outed by society. i
love their resistance

I'll tell you something personal, my friend (in an email, so always beware, the jumping wild words, the play within). The quick surprise of love is not dead in any of us, I do hope.

Given what I love about words, I love interacting with Neil: his way of being in the world, his form of communication, the relationship between materiality and meaning in his emails, and, of course, dancing with him. And it all was just great, really enjoyable (and still is).

Neil was clearly having a fantastic time, with lots of people, but he did behave quite differently towards me, and my friends teased me about it, so it was plenty noticeable. But it was clear to me that he is an amazing flirt, a magnetic personality, and so I kept myself nicely safe there.

But then, towards of the end of his stay here, he kissed me. Oh, it was so lovely. I hadn't been kissed by another man for fourteen years, and it was quite a spectacular kiss, very surprising, very intimate, naked, under cloth banners, with the others only a red silk membrane away. And I felt everything a fourteen year old feels, but with a lot more experience. Of course I am not fourteen, and so I did ask him a while later via email about what was up, and he told me: no, he felt no attraction or desire towards me, and the kiss, which was lovely for both of us, was a celebration of the joy of that moment. Fair enough (sigh). It's ok, and put away as a one-off bounded event, but wow, let me share with you the delight of that moment. I'll look forward to working with Neil in the future, and enjoying the language/movement things, and his wonderful facility with touch.

But what a lovely thing to have happened, once, and for me to remember so vividly: an amulet, and we need those, too. I share it with you, as that: something for luck.

dear petra..
my days are dreary im sad to say
i wake up blank and mad
at my life and health
i feel powerless and lost
thats whats going on
perhaps caused by 3 major surgeries since 2000
perhaps its the war

thanks.neil
for listening

i had fun in michigan

Statue

Caught in polished stone
hard shell of an old egg
rubbed the crocodile eye
scarred shark dry tooth
once emu feather float

shine high
light thin
oh pedestal zoo coat
grand matter turn
turn away the hand,
hand, my hand.

Wet clay land
melt in the open pool
sink to you, sand
down, warmer
soft cobra belly
leopard coat close

cracks appear out
in the air
skin cushion coat
longer bubble
blisters peel wet lips

lips, my lips
lick tissue

in play
elephant ear flick
now hard art
pull it over me
here, grey tender
go to sleep

Blood warm hollow
generosity of sand:
wait for time to grind
wait for a hand to fall silent
wait for the movement of Gaia
wait for the skin to be dust
wait for the dust to be clay
wait for the water
wait for the warmth of the tallow candle
wait for the light of the bones
in the heat of your furnace, fire me.

Touch me now, grain to grain
voice to voice
form without form
memory without time
wet rustle moves marble in my hand.

the elephants...the whole natural world is watching over
us.
i cant imagine why steven hawkings wants to live in outer
space
can we teach him
emu eyed wonder
do you fear black holes?
how many pomegranate seeds have you eaten?
sending hugs
neil

Poems are my pomegranate seeds, to look into the dark
with. Imagine touching the belly of a snake. And the
comfort of elephants.

I shall come to you, once for every seed you feed me:
sweet between my lips, and hardness peeled
and in my robe I bring flowers: white waxy arum lilies,
stiff and perfect to hold on to the light
I left behind: to keep the flame at night,
to remind us of the lightness of a feather,
of the dove that flew up,
of the old tree, torn asunder by electric storms,
of the embrace of the bear who roams,
of the taste of honey, deep,
and of those bee stings
as I leave, dear friend, you yet again behind.

for every seed you savor
you will come with me to my world for a time
and you will lose all connection with reason and live in
wild satyrical laughter of le
bateau ivre
as you peer on the edge of time

come petra.........

But seeds can take hold, unfold, and open up a canopy.
Will you hold me like an oak? Tend me, with peacock
feathers, and I will bathe you in oils of tender plants,
aromas of the field, opiates of a summer dream that
rides us past the rivers of tomorrow.
But when we wake, might we find our hands entwined,
sturdy roots of winter?

petra....................
can you feel my mind at work?
it fences with every neutron surrounding i
and lunges and plucks in laughter
every stayed idea.
i think i doth have vision

If your hand does not move,
let the nerves of the air knit a web
if your shoulder does not shrug,
let the carpet of your breath unroll for a magic ride
if your back does not bend,
may the earth heave up to bring us close
if your cheek does not feel mine,
let words murmur like tender hairs bent by sun wind
may the beads in your lung hear, the beat of your heart
sing,
the valves open with the rhythm of touch,
blood dance,
tissue sigh,
bones dream,
the circle wheeling: our breaths travel the star distances,
molecules surf on the moisture between planets,
to feel, to feel in a tenderness of light,
to spark light blue in a brain that knows no boundary, at
night, behind closed eyes:
and there is the sense of it all.

Persephone sits in the dark.
Wind, thunder hunch over me.
Darkness rent by lighting, nothing illuminates.
Black branches whip through and through.
I feel the mist damp on my skin.
Deep in my mind, a spark glows warm,
red smell, lilac taste.
Touch the sinews of my spine,
relax, unravel, and uncoil my form.
Memory glows outward,
a lamp in my flesh.
The shades find me,
a candle in the dark.
Come to me, wayfarer: there is room, here,
and shelter.

Landscape

Kuppers and Marcus

whenever I see people arguing or fighting with issues
i always see the truth behind it
a desire to be heard and loved
deeply
i try my best to live by this knowledge
in it
with it
you have heard me many times
it is love
i hope i hear you too
CATZzzzzzzzzzzzzzzzzzzzzzzzzzzzzzzzzzzzzzzzzzzz
PURRRRRRRRRRRRRRRRRRRRRRRRRRRRRRRRRRRRRR

Oh, you hear me, Neil. Even when I do not speak. That's
why we are in this conversation, no? I love that you
hear me - but also how you hear me, the different
sounds you hear, the notes I hear of myself when I
open my voices to you, and when I hear yours, and
how those unfold in my ear, and how body and sound
and hearing and touching come together. Our emails,
you to me, me to you: this is such a satisfying communication to me. Including the moments when we do
not hear each other, when there is so much more to
explore.

A purring kiss back to you (and I hear your sound, your
purr, right now: even if that purr might be not without
costs to you)

yes i see the sadness and longing
to be desired and truly loved. and sexually too?
for me i do not often let the love in(which is another
story)
...
im sure you have seen and felt wonders in your life
it shows
..but on a deep level..loneliness?
i can but see you snowing in a warm pool with a bit or
bite of float
and two life guards telling you to and not to
carry me to the pools edge.
hugs ..neil

On a deep level, loneliness seems inevitable.

I assume/imagine/project onto you that you have much
more occasion to think about the dis-connect of words,
gesture, dance. Dance is not a remedy: but it is a
bridge, a different one from words.

I send you the warm silky touch of my two cats, both
sitting on my knees right now.

(UCSF) THE ART OF COMMUNICATION
Devva Kasnitz (uc berkeley) and Russell Shuttleworth
[EDITED BY NEIL MARCUS]
An assumption of fluent spoken human speech is very close to an anthropological universal. A society may place more or less value on non-spoken communication, but not to replace voice. I THINK DANCE MIGHT BE INCLUDED HERE. Our acceptance of sign language as language is precisely because so many of its characteristics also exist in spoken communication. ALL SOCIETIES HAVE DANCE AS AN INTEGRAL PART OF THEM. COULD DANCE BE AS IMPORTANT AS SPEECH. ISNT TOUCH THE BASIS OF DANCE AND ALL COMMUNICATION.
I TOUCH YOU WITH MY WORDS WITH MY PRESANCE WITH MY BEING WITH MY ESSANCE. The textual analysis of oral discourse is a vital part of sociolinguistics BUT IT ISNT E V E R Y T H I N G . A prejudicial hierarchy of disability plagues the disability rights movement. This hierarchy was and is usually based on appearance and on spoken communication, AND ABILITY TO MOVE WITH EASE. AS I HAVE LEARNED THO, ANYBODY CAN DANCE. Movement leaders AND DANCE COLLABORATORS are making very conscious efforts to mitigate this process.

:-). Looks like we are stepping into an exciting and existing conversation here. Funny that we are using so many words and concepts in tandem: I don't think that you had mentioned 'non-verbal communication' as a word to me: but right when I met you, that seemed to me what your abilities are about: combining and thinking about the relationship between different communication modes.

I agree that dance is a significant part of communication, and I think it is part of verbal communication, too. Poetry, for instance, is to me so much about the movement of tongue and throat and lungs, at least when I write and perform it. All writing is movement to me, all movement closely related to writing and speaking. And to put arbitrary rules over that, parceling it out into right and wrong: well, that's the complex bit. I think there are words in eyes, and eyes in words. And thoughts without words, colors without names, emotions which can't be contained by sentences.

We'll have fun working on all this. Maybe, if you are interested, when you feel well, we can schedule a day or so, and just email back and forth, short bits, writing collaboratively about these things and our knowledges, making our different voices resonant? You can write something short, and I can respond, expand, and you can then edit me, write into my words: a poetic collaboration where I will try to listen to all you are saying, you listen to me, and we can see if that is a good working method that does not tire you too much. We'll find a way. Of course, I'd like to do it in your presence, my hand in yours, or me touching your back while you type, finding a good balance between relaxation and control.

hi petra
;-) in my state
economy with precision is key
heart core image feeling touch speak
or
just touch speak
i gaze et al
observe
fine tune
with fear too and doubt
that i cant afford
;-);-);-);-);-);-);-);-);-);-);-)
i must have exorbitant amounts of fun
b l i m e y

Balance on the carousel
a carnival of fun
carne vale: beware the flesh, heart core,
or hard rock café
where music rocks you around the clock
listen closely into the bars of steel
that hold you, secure, in your seat,
that keep gravity at bay
that dance in their old old rhythm
then slip out from under, feel the steel
touch the dangerous leather
fear the fall, doubt the ground:
speak with the red red tongue
of a rolling stone.
Here, on the ground, I look up:
I fear, for you, feel the fall, and see you fly,
ride on the wind. Do not leave me
behind.

.........and you Petra, i think, are asking me to stand up on the rrollercoaster and feel the wind

i also am feeling tremendously articulate in ways i can hardly imagine

my body has been a remarkable teacher..and you...the wind?

love neil

I am. That's what I say... we am, us are, being/you, I: living.

I find you tremendously articulate, indeed, gracile, performative, dancerly. With line breaks, and silences, and graphic marks as well as words. White space/black space. A poet, in an Augenblick, a wink. Is it strange to you that I only know you now? Do you not think of yourself as articulate in quite the same way as you were before your operations?

id love to lay with you
in sun in hot shade
in water
....anywhere...........
and talk of memories and sailing ships
xx00xx and hugs

you float
on my soft body
suspended in spring-fed water
iron brown below

small bird skeleton
on the beach, bleached
needles curve up
a crown of gentle thorns

muscled palm
on my white breast
fingernail traces an aureole
sun dogs dip down

old bones grow green
twigs and hollow tubes
whistle in the wind:
what do you remember

touched
how do you fill all air?
how do we fly?
we move marked by our blood
we move open to the wind
we move in the bone
what sails our bodies make

i tremble now

a kiss,a moan,an ahhhhhh,an ouch
a more,or less a touch,a rub, a slither
a please, a show me..tell me true
its all unknown as yet
or how far we want
must talk.must feel and smell and touch.
oh god love.what is it? i always ask

oh petra,

how fragile the heart is
tho i try hard to make mine not
thats why i dont fall easily
or expect too much
but i can say i am kind and giving
and dont want to hurt you at all...
....
a gentle spank tho
neil

How about a heart as wide and mobile as an octopus?
Arms reach out through breasts and spines,
caress, twist, touch fire and all elements:
pulled in, pulled out, pulsing
uncoil this somersault
this cycle of embrace
and find some space:
salty waters moisten thin membranes
salty tissues reach and swell
salty tears leave rivers on the skin
pathways where eels swim.
All swim, I swim, forward and out, loop the loop
to the coral reefs and the blue ocean.

I am salmon
Somewhere in my waking dreams there is a memory of
a spiral walkway that slopes downward going past an
underwater pool with windows in it.

As we're walking around and it starts to pour rain, I
notice we're at the seattle aquarium
so...lets go in.

in 1968 I came to seattle to get counseling. I was having a rough time accepting myself and being in the
world. All confused... love,longing,fear and hiding. My
father was into a peer counseling called rc which was
based in seattle and was very supportive. I got out of
school for a week and agreed to try it out.
719 2nd ave north
visit there if you can

first came the salmon exhibit. Salmon are born and
grow up here and are released into the ocean here
..and find their way back here to spawn and begin the
new generation.

When I came here for counselling, one day I woke up. A
counsellor just simply loved me and suddenly I think I
realized that I was lovable and had love too to give.

ive been here before. I always felt a pull to return here
tho I didnt quite kno why. Now I know.
I think my dad took me to this aquarium in 1968 and I
think I walked in public here for the first time. I was
born under the sea here. Looking out into the deep.

I just woke up hot
dream body circle all one
your arms touch my skin
xxxooo
p

I hear your kisses quite clearly
and hear us say ummmmmmmmmmmm and ahhhhhhhhhh
and i kiss you back as my lips are my most curious
appendage
and yes ALFREDO OR MARINARA is good
as good as green algae
or oysters
i love sushi
but most of all i love sitting closer than youll see anybody sit.

a poem of kssess
clik.tick.tak.shhh.smmm.
hummmm.llllllllllllllll.iiiiiiiiiiiiiiiiiiiiii.aaaaaaaaaa.
tickle swish,puck,poooh.and slide.
bathe in it all.
talk.stories.write history
make love in cool
rest sleep.
up and greet
hi honey
its a new day........................with no pressure other than our
warm circulations
and pumping fluids
;-)

So good talking with you on IM. I am hanging out at home, waiting for the car to become available, and for two builders to show up to give me quotes on adding a shower downstairs, widening the bathroom door, and adding a ramp to the back door. The ramp and door access will definitely be done for your visit in September - I am not as sure about the shower as about the rest, but we'll work with it. You will definitely have access to a loo and a basin downstairs and the hottub outside. And there is always a water hose, if the shower should not be installed yet. And we can go to the local swimming pool, too, if the lake is too cold at that time. But you run hot, my love, and I have a thick European skin for swimming in colder lakes, so we'll be fine. Last year, Lisa and I were swimming until October 9th! But no worries, in all likelihood, the shower will be in place.

I'll go swimming later. Life is good, I swim each day in our lake, and look forward with warm delight to being together. I wish I could marry Berkeley's attractions to the Michigan lakes, and the summery, golden and lush land here.

i feel this joy of our joy
of seeing and feeling and loving the joy
and wide eyed trembling notations
i luv looking at you as i ....
or you..........................
or we ....
its a dance like none other
DANCE OF THE OTHER
creative kamasutra krip cryptics
calicentriccriptoeroticas

if theres doubt in my voice
its a lot about my self perceived bodily limitations
in an unsureworld
love....i do not doubt

i thought of swimming
in YOUR lake
everday
i just hav to get there

kneil my love
i shall anoint thee
;-)

i was with the trees one hr ago !
and i devised a plan for us
to create a "makeout at the oaks day"
we,of course would be the lead couple
i met tinkerbell a tree sitter there today
and a guy who said he was a bounty hunter
i also peed in my pants
its a good day
miss u lovehoneysweetheartpartner

Neil had phoned me the day after the Anarcha symposium, as I was lying in bed, dog-tired, and had asked me to come out to dance in his hotel pool. I went, and brought one of Lisa's underwater cameras. Yesterday, I had a first occasion to look in detail at the shots I took that day.

I also had a very upsetting experience yesterday, alone. It was just one of those misunderstandings, no one to blame, but I had become separated from my friends during a Nomad concert in Ann Arbor's Summer Festival. In the midst of the summer night revelers, I had stayed put for over an hour, awaiting the return of two parties of friends. Then I had tried to walk amongst the crowd, trying to find them: a hopeless undertaking, and I was just jostled by strangers, my knees giving way, music changing to noise in my ear as I was beginning to feel helpless. I sat down again, on the grass, for a short while, and thought of the pool images.

Neil floats in green water, he drifts past the camera. Buoyancy and muscle power are at odds with one another, as he tries to achieve suspension, and forces around him break it. I push the camera down, push my own body beneath the waters in order to photograph from below, try to angle the camera at this other body, near me, capture shadows and light. We will ourselves to enter this different element and yet capture the freedom of water, where we both move without pain. There are moments of delicious drift. For seconds, we are at stillness, with held breath. Our muscular limbs darting down into the water are no longer awkward. Hope.

At the concert, I assumed everybody had gone home, all assuming that I was with the respective other party. Independence was out of my crip reach. Loneliness fell over me: in the past weeks, I had driven around Berkeley with a powerchair, enjoying the freedom and lack of pain. Two weekends before that, I had been in our Tiresias performance shoot with my old manual chair, enjoying its comfortable familiar presence. Now, I was not only a tri-pedal completely at odds with the locomotion and ease of the summer festival, I was also on my own in Ann Arbor in ways I have not been before, and found myself unprepared for the challenge.

A fish out of water. Tiresias, the Greek male/female seer, stepping with her staff: another pain crip with whom I can share the exhaustion of insufficient access, the pain of the step, the walk, the density of movement, my painful limbs, my cane, my knees that scream to stop. Shapeshift into another element: the lightness of movement in water, suspension. But it requires effort, and preparation, to meet new elements, to find an alchemy of connection. Bring the bathing suit (in a public place, anyway). Bring an underwater camera. Prepare to hold your breath. Know what you have to do. Find a way to float. Achieve suspension. Know that will stop, and you will have to try again.

Of course it all turned out well at the concert: my friends phoned me eventually, and found me as I was sitting on the pavement away from the concert. It's a pretty familiar experience: being left somewhere where access is not great. I cannot circulate as a standing, walking person. And when I get too tired, I cannot tolerate loud all-encompassing sound. And sometimes I forget to keep myself safe. Or to just enjoy the feeling of being unsafe, of giving myself over, knowing that it will be okay, no need to panic, it's all going to work out. No one but myself can help with that one: finding trust.

In the pool, Neil took a deep breath, and dived under. I took a deep breath, and dived under. The beauty of limbs in a choreography of pulls: float and power, will and abeyance, the muscles of arm, neck, back. Bodies in unusual constellation, unsafe safety.

Today, the day after the Nomad concert, I feel awkward: I hope I have not made my friends uncomfortable with my strange panic. I am also in pain, knees and hips screaming at me from all the walking. I long to float. Or, rather, maybe, I long for that muscular exertion without chaffing, the exploration of a different ele- ment, a world with different gravitational rules where bodies can drift past one another with grace.

These thoughts do not come together neatly, wrapped up into an argument, as I am still shaken by my real- ization what living alone in Ann Arbor, without con- stant back-up support, can mean for me. Melodrama or drama, I need to either relax or find better ways of sorting myself out. But all the photos help: Lisa's black and white ones of me as a strong and beautiful woman, among a tribe of gorgeous people. These pool photos of the strange elation of being in a different ele- ment, a different kind of safety. Tiresias does not just speak about comfort, as we've all been finding out in many different ways. She does not speak about a stable position at all: he's speaking from his own tri-pedal position, an imbalance of limbs on earth, a limp in the olive grove. Effort, oracle, instability, lack of clarity: giving oneself to the transformations that are inevitable, and enjoying the ride. We'll see what movement grace I can find in this slip-stream. These images of Neil swimming show me some of our elegance. Together, we can live not always comfortably, but artfully.

i love your juxta positioning.i use that a lot.maybe its the way brains work.......compare/contrast

i want a partner
to share life with
amazing life

we will lead and follow each other thru the morass

are you scared about the trip?me?love?
maybe
i think it will be ok
im hopeful
we'll talk
and love each other thru fear

I am packed. All is organized. No, I wasn't scared of life
at your end
I am scared of myself, sometimes, my limitations
I get scared when I cannot work it out
when I get numb
when I get lazy
when I just lie on my bed for the day,
drugged, dull, dull, dull
and I can't hear you
and I can't hear myself
when all is thick around me:
the fog of pain

I am NOT scared of being with you
I am NOT scared of love
but I sometimes worry that I am not what you see ...
not all that strong...
not all that clever...
but that worry goes away: you know more than that

Pain is loneliness
and worthlessness
and tiredness
and lack of life
but something new is opening up out of it

everyday the fog comes in and goes out
theres always a breeze at high noon
the postman rings at 11 and four
at nite sax practices next door
garbage trucks circulate the alleys every morning
glad to get a thumbs up
love

Disability Culture

Dear friends,

I am writing to you since I doubt that I will find the time to speak with you today. Neil and I are together in Berkeley.

This is neil speaking,
I see and feel we have similar poetics and joy of life.we egg eachother on in the modalities of love.most satisfying and touchably real......

And this is Petra
Indeed ☺. It's quite a journey we are embarking on. Our first date was the Disability Film Festival, and the first film we saw (totally by chance) was Steve Kuusisto's Planet of the Blind, shot by a German filmmaker. It was very moving to me: listening to the poetry of a friend while exploring being near to Neil. Wow. And after the films, the cinema was filled with people Neil knew – and I knew. We've got dates set up all over the place.
Next date-stop: restaurant, poetry scribbled on the paper table cover, delicious food.

The last film we saw was about the polio epidemic in den-mark in the 50's.not the best makeout movie in the world..........but kisses seemed very appropriate.....neil

Will you still love me
If I
Deposit celery
On
Your...
Bosom

pk (5:03:48 PM): what is disability culture?

neilmarcus (5:10:04 PM): i used that term way back.it seemed the only way to bring art into the otherwise 'medical' conversation. i thought art was the way to bridge the gap...i worked.art.poetry.spirit love=the grat sustainers of a peopleINSTANTLY RECOGNIZABLE

pk (5:12:28 PM): what about today? Do you not think that the term allows for an umbrella, a rallying point for younger artists today? And does the term not also allow us to create an aesthetic separate from the tired 'outsider art' label?

neilmarcus (5:14:32 PM): DEFINATELY YES. CULTURE IS AS STONG A WORD AS THERE IS. DISABILITY IS MUCH DEEPER THAN A LIFESTYLE

pk (5:15:10 PM): yes

pk (5:15:50 PM): what do we hold open when we claim the word? What is shared across the many different forms of embodiment that disability culture artists have?

neilmarcus (5:15:54 PM): who can argue that we do not dance

neilmarcus (5:16:30 PM): or reach for stars

neilmarcus (5:17:00 PM): crips in space evenn

pk (5:17:21 PM): what are the dangers of claiming disability culture?

neilmarcus (5:18:02 PM): we longggg for a higher view of disability

neilmarcus (5:20:37 PM): patient client consumer those are words for rubes were way past rubes in our land.

neilmarcus (5:21:14 PM): were the future

neilmarcus (5:21:52 PM): we are the past and present.

pk (5:22:29 PM): but plenty of people think that calling for a shared culture is the wrong way to go about empowerment. create a form of They want to expand the non-disabled world, not counter-culture. What do you think about that?

neilmarcus (5:22:43 PM): we dont e ve n kno how much

neilmarcus (5:24:13 PM): let me see their plan.their vision

pk (5:25:54 PM): that seems to me the problem: their plan or vision is indivdiualised, only extends to one individual body/person/entity at a time.

neilmarcus (5:25:57 PM): counterculture? were all 'different'

pk (5:27:28 PM): but disability culture has counter-cultural elements, I find.

pk (5:27:49 PM): the fact that there is not one thing that unites us is also our strength: and it can show in our aesthetics.

neilmarcus (5:31:43 PM): variety is the key concept.no people can fit one mold .we offer a very unique angle on the lifes questions

West coast contact improv festival...

I am not easy with the word crip. still. but I'll use it here
as shorthand...
We were crips at this contact festival.
They were thrilled to have us as some of their focus
was 'mixed abilities" an awful term in my mind.
Reminds me of dog breeding.

They were very interested in being sensitive to the
needs of crips. but they ended up being so 'careful and
'sensitive' it was very irritating. And I felt very insulted.
yuck ! and excluded anyway
With the giant accessible portapotty at the front door.
Bad feng shway.

There was a big jam performance nearing the end of
the fest. Me and petra in the midst of all the other
dancers crawling all over and doing improvy things like
pretending to be punk robots or wavy wavy trees and
snakes with attitude.

In our contact dance improv as part of the final group
performance piece, petra and I decided we would
spend the time kissing. which we did while everybody
else was "dancing". Ah yes kissing.
High art. radical Art. reminiscent of sex onstage in the
60's.

Was it a bizarre script or what. And it made petra laugh.
It was a kind of laugh like an lsd trip. it made me laugh

too. laughing wildly and kissing at and in a 'dance' performance. We were being 'bad' crips. Indulging ourselves, our sex, our bodies in full sight of the audience.
Ha ha ha. After it was over I left the scene quickly.
When I woke up the next morning I felt very ashamed. I
was 'bad' I had insulted everyone in the room (I thought)

How strange to feel that as I had felt 'insulted' all day.
Why did I suddenly turn on
myself for executing a novel idea. a beautiful idea such
as a kiss.

There are two beds in my room
One, the more recent is a hospital bed
I hate its image in my mind
With all its connotations

The other is a hand made wooden bed
Carved by my brother out of maple
Using no nails
Its queen sized

I was almost ready to get rid of it
Its big…after all my bedroom is my theater room as well
with its own stage and curtain
Whats the point
Im old etc.

And then you came into my life
A perfect meeting place for you and I
Before bedtime after lunch after waking…anytime 4am.

My nest is important to me
What luck!

What if this world were a four-poster bed
and we the seafarers on an adventure larger than the
moon?
Beyond the silk
only bored sharks, drowned mermen
and the hustle of the small fry.
As the curtains wave around our forms,
we excavate, mould, shape a new island,
we lick clay into shape.
Moon rain: let's grow aqualungs
and corals will bloom for us,
variegated flowers in the milky night.

4 posted bed in the sea
how lovely
to chart this voyage
with my poet lover

Did we not feel like royalty
2 fast smooth chariots powered by electric servos
whizzing in and out of crowds
thru gates and pillars
hot on each others tails
so different from our public
watching us
watch them
easily laugh
I see you
Weaving
In and out
Thrilling ride
Fast for audience with our king

Velvet green embraces as we sink
skin smooth, a link to a Jurassic age
saurian mellow, languid role through the dark
mark the protuberances, cool, fellow feeling
drowned in the wet face world of strangers
touch, sink, nip and touch again,
asserting companionship. But in the main,
buoyancy disrupts the pas-de-deux:
you sail into the green growth, me cartwheel
to the lily pads. Oil and tears of water.
A floater, coming up for air: hiss in my ear,
an inelegant kiss opens the flower

Now I am tired
A drooping wilted rose
brown, crisp, at the edges
juices do not flow unhindered
but deep inside there's red
river running
silver flash fish on the waters
green memory
sturdy stem waits
for the drought to end
for the rain
to fly over the garden.

Bit under the weather here... IT'S HOT!
will go to the movies with Lisa, watch some silly stuff
in air conditioning
love you.

doesnt heat slow down time, he asks
yes not unlike pain
making you watch the moment
of automatic elevators travels up and down
sleek,cool shafts of forgotten darkness

replies with kisses attached to cool washcloths

my tiresian journey

maybe they would have called me a spastic mute in
ancient times
I am spastic
Meaning
I dance
My muscles dance
..all the time and act as if weightlifting
..all the time (except when I sleep or swim or laf or cry)
mute, I kind of like mute
its like muse
A muse.
What does he who rarely speaks and yet who seems to
have so many "voices"
Who chooses his word so carefully and economically
What does HE think ? ?
What is HIS View of the world
I feel like an oracle
Looking so closely, watching the world
Thinking about it
Loving it sooo much
Loving my perspective
What I can offer
And I do look different, dancing all the time
What's that like ?
Curious
We all want to know what THIS life has to offer
hmmmmmmmmmmmmmmmmmmmmmmm

what happens when the muse speaks, when poet and muse are one, and the one enters into dialogue, and kisses become poems, and dancing happens across one body and another, and moves? what happens when the one in pain speaks about pain, and still does not claim to know what pain can be in language? I love this post. I shall reply later, first, off to sushi with Aimee.
I love you, too.

i attempt to kno everything and ive learned a lot
from my body
what do i kno?
hug me
hear my muted words
love me
let me love you

THE MUTE SPEAKS in MANY TONGUES
Art
Touch
Whispers
Tones
Oh excuse me, I just got a call from the us navel
reserve; they hung up quickly after
asking how I was
I was mute
I usually don't answer the phone
My speech is garbled to the untrained 'ear'
My other mother tongues are extremely clear
Dance
Laughter
Love
Hope
The whirling of thought
Gaze/sight/feelsmelltaste
there are so many languages to talk in
at the barber today
she was very joyful to talk with me with her limited
English
smiles say a lot
she was very cheered to kno I knew the number of the
clipper length guard comb to use

love you love you love you love you love you love you
love you love you love you love you love you love
youlove you love you love you love love love you love
you love you love you love you love you love you love
youlove you love you love you love you love you love
you love you love you love you love you love you love
youlove you love you love you love you love you love
you love you love love love you love you love you love
youlove you love you love you love you love you love
love love love love you love you love you love you you
love youlove you love you love you love you love you
love you love you love you love you love you love you
love youlove you love you love you love you love you
love you love you love you love you love you love you
you love youlove you love you love you love you love
you love you love you love you love you love you you
you love youlove you love you love you love you love
you love you love you love you love love love you love
you love youlove you love you love you love you love
love you love you love you love you love you love you
love you love youlove you you you love you love you
love you love you love you love you love you love you
love you love youlove you love you love you you you
you love you love you love you love you love you love
you love you love youlove you love you love you love
you love you love you love you love you love you love
love you love you love youlove you love you love you
love you love you love you love you love you love you
love you love you love youlove you love you love you
love you love you love you love you love you love you
love you love you love youlove you love you love you

i realize i have lots to say about bodies. feldenkrais communicated to me that it didnt matter how twisted i was he was gonna straighten me out.he defied me. i think that's what all people are looking for someone who defies their alienation. whatever form that alienation takes. we cant really understand eachother with linear language.its also difficult to understand ourselves.weve learned from society to deny much of who we are or suppress it. moshe talked to me about the scots who toss logs for fun with names that have a mc-before every family. We learn thru play.and thru people.one of my favorite quotes goes something like this ONE HUMAN BRAIN [NERVOUS SYSTEM] FEELS MOST AT HOME WITH ANOTHER.its simplicity and complexity is most attractive. .we communicate thru play.life is a dance. dance is play. touch is love.love is play. therapy is play.a game of wits. the best therapy is improvised play. probably,the best therapists are the kids on the street. or the baby who grasps your thumb.that touch is truly the touch of god. and when it works well,its usually a great big funny,make no sense joke. life is a joke.its a joke were alive. we dont even know why.

hi dear its 915 pm
and i had to tell my roommate to go out
leave me with my joyful memories
of
our first 'date'
i love you
neil
talk soon
smell soon
touch soon
again
my love

Fool Fog
Wing-hollow warm
I fly
nestle like a heavy   feather
lift breath whistle
kiss tether
I sail
to you

pirouette my nightmare in this mayday
rite
find your storm   blanket

good night out we glide
albatross farewell to the land quilt
night rhythm soft rhyme
your fine skin parchment cipher in my ear

What stories in the wind sing?

murmur shell
your wine-dark seas
your blue pool
our lake still moon water
I hover

morning ravels the wave
fool fog driftwood
flotsam scrape   my nerve
our skin
and still we press on
and build
and build
with water
with waves
ice fire caves

        your touch whole
in the breath as we swing
                    we swing
        swing out into our sun

merrywhistle milkwood
step dancing
crying loons

our swing our reach
is grand
extensive
beyond sight
far out
cool
and nervey

but easy as that feather hollow

watching harry potter is useful. world inside a world
a cracking egg
a still
a gaze
a look
butohesque life
meaning
;-)

neilmarcus (11:34:55 AM): my pain support group yesterday
neilmarcus (11:35:09 AM): fantastic me
pk (11:36:18 AM): ?
neilmarcus (11:37:52 AM): being a revolutionary talking about sort of deaf president now politics sex and cripdom.pain authority control focault
pk (11:38:30 AM): yes, oh yes. I see that.
neilmarcus (11:38:46 AM): and they lit up.i set the room ablaze
pk (11:38:50 AM): sex-positive politics
pk (11:39:08 AM): the caped crusader, indeed
neilmarcus (11:39:33 AM): in our group needed saying...with pain too
neilmarcus (11:40:04 AM): many tongues yes
neilmarcus (11:40:35 AM): alternate tongues
pk (11:40:54 AM): that would be something for poetry: pain and eros, not self-induced pain, but how there's something about the experience of pain in another body that is so intimate, links people so closely ... I am aware of your pain when we make love, somewhat... and my own.
pk (11:41:37 AM): tongues - in what language?
neilmarcus (11:41:38 AM): its only a little
pk (11:41:57 AM): well, there are different pains?
neilmarcus (11:42:51 AM): the other mother tongue a book on gay history i saw her speak
pk (11:44:06 AM): ok, ok. I love the connection, and to gay history, too.
neilmarcus (11:44:15 AM): yes pain of speech loss
pk (11:44:30 AM): yes
pk (11:44:38 AM): pain of disconnect
neilmarcus (11:44:47 AM): movement loss
neilmarcus (11:45:11 AM): fear/pain
pk (11:45:13 AM): pain of invisibility, non-fitting, anchorless

pk (11:45:37 AM): pain of loneliness
neilmarcus (11:45:37 AM): gender pain
neilmarcus (11:46:16 AM): separateness pain
pk (11:47:10 AM): pain of sadness
neilmarcus (11:47:51 AM): ok poem of pain? yes and joy
pk (11:48:42 AM): yes, poems out of pain are about con-
nect, love, joy, fullness, being heard, reaching towards
understanding
neilmarcus (11:49:03 AM): i love you
pk (11:49:22 AM): I love you

a seduction of fear

i am afraid of you
because you are bold and beautiful
i think i hide embarrassment alot
therefore
i would like to let mine out with you
laf/horror
at what i might say or do
?

dear petra
i am
we are
all struck by the ravages of War
and still we reach
for stars.......

touch this hand, make it valuable
touch this shoulder, relax into warmth
touch this neck, release to bloom
touch my lips with yours, tickle breath
cradle my head, let me rest only rest
cradle my spine, bend like a waterfall
cradle my hips, unfold like a lotus
cradle my knees, dullness washed with the silver of love
let my mind dissolve into you
with the surf, ebb and flow,
neural energy
passion's fruit
a collective of skin
let me drink your pain
sip of mine
familiar taste wine in our mouths

IM SO HAPPY.TO SEE YOU
SHARE MY LIFE
LOVE YOU
WRITE YOU
CREATE
PLAY
SING
SMELL
TASTE
HOLD
FEEL
ARC YOU
BATHE YOU
SWIM
TRAVEL
EAT
;-)
;-)
;-)
;-)
;-)
;-)
;-)
;-)
;-)
;-)

The gaps in cyber-space become tactile to me, and I feel what I am missing.

I was down yesterday: traveling, as much as I do it and like it, takes a lot out of me, is hard on my bones, and pain creates distances.
Here is my last poem. It still feels quite raw, but at times, that is not a bad thing.

Night Visitors
        For Karen Fiser

You want to know what it is like?
My fingers curl, beckoning I know not what.
What distills here in my blood?

Compounds of tree bark, spicy pepper, codeine,
magic leg positions disturbed by ant feet, mechanical
imagination un-done by an animal kingdom
too wild, too fleet, herds in my capillary veins,
un-killable, un-dead, their passage leaves
a savannah of ghost bed sheets,
empty blanket roar.

The drama of it all: it sings
a workers' chorus just beneath my skin,
bass bone vibrates a tendon,
anatomy trance symphony,
x-visioned clarity un-matched by starlight.

It aches, Jim, but not as we know it.
To listen, really listen, to this pain,
dissolves long after tears,
leaves body parts strewn across the bed
where red shirts walk on a new planet, chart a course:
It does un-gather, voids the joints of
knee, hip, shoulder, finger, skull:
lines un-drawn, spider's web of loud nerve cocoons
these words, well cushioned, moth-eaten support.

You want to know the tune?
Battlestar Galactica space opera,
Commander Adama, stay, for me.
Grand dreams, and a narrow harrow
etches poems I cannot remember,
forgettable essays that drown in the pillow,
epistles un-send. Un-heard music.

You want to know the story?
Words must act. Heathcliff sobs,
hits a shin on the barren mountaintop of the night.
The credits roll on the Ponderosa Ranch,
Spock has no answer and bleeds green,
Johnny Weissmuller clings to his vine.

dearest dear petra,
PAIN IS PART OF US.not just a
dreaded word. it is an opening
it is-in my words- a birth.
i feel much love here as well as defiance of convention
i feel 2001 intelligence
origins
thus spoke Zarathustra
tarzan was my dear companion
the spices and herbs make me feel connected
love and more love
with the feet of ants...

necessity of creating our own language
since there is no other than our own to be accurate.
it is self described
built on self knowledge
the only? true power
there is......
WOW.its magnitude
it reaches far
p.s. big earthquake 430 am friday

i have many friends who have died
lonely disabled people
i cherish our connection
beyond all sadness
and in spite of pain
we soar
and MAKE love
im lucky to have found you

Night Ice

Storm roared joints carol
snow angels in my bed
move my bones
into the white whirl

midnight ball bearing
off to the sleep pillow
to the maw
        night lion's claws

sing over the window
into the white whirl
path clad in crystal armor
lances into the door
at knee fall

to the fingertip
song drift
whiter in the ice air

tonight it is ten degrees outside
in the mirror, I hold a blue pill
one, two, maybe three and I lay down
out on my porch
go to sleep
blue princess
veins like ice flowers

slow crunch of the ice lion
mumbling to his pride
in the thaw of the moon
rock this marble heart

if I hold a cat in each hand,
will I fly?

will you still love me
if I do not get that rock chick gig
on Mars
?

i will love you
if you were motionless
in a coal pit...

I'll try to listen through the fog of my chattering thoughts.

I sit on the edge
here's the continent's foggy end
no horizon limit
no wall and no brick
seal's elegant fluke rises to me
an arch stitches water and air
swims a liquid ocean quilt
I breathe sea salt:
new beginnings
a journey as old as the sky
seen by eyes that know delight in the other
touched by your skin lapping the coast
a salty dissolve

why do old tears float me away?
for words halt the drift
mark the land of our paradise
stake a claim in the waters of time
we are here
I hold your touch in me
your voice in my ear
we embroider the bed of our future

at the waters edge
i sit with you
watch the horizon, sun set
happy i am
with salty tears
and embroidered dreams
as we slowly, like beavers
build our homes to stand off the floods
of rushing streams overflow

our breath mingle
our lips trace the midnight map
know our certainty
I sleep in the warm shadow
of that map: it knows more than I do
shares the wisdom of you and me
shows the way
to our hospitable castle
in which our balls will ring with laughter
in which our friends will toast and sparkle
in which we dance tangos and waltzes
in which we sing with the nightingales
in which we roar with the waves
in which we hold hands with the world
in which we will rest, each night,
having found our way, again,
to the midnight map
that knows us well.

We will share the map
in the pages of books and the art of life
we will knit our map with other people's,
laid side by side like the AIDS quilt,
to cushion the feet and wheels of our fellows,
support a movement that builds the land of
our culture,
our future

In our weakness, in our fears,
we consult the growing map
and see the contours of disabled country
as our home
our comfort

our warmth
fears of death and isolation
melt in the glow of our life
hot golden pearls around which we accrete
the jewels of our castle
an alchemy: pain and laughter, tenderness

All can dance through our castle:
blind, and deaf, with singular steps,
with singular voices
and beautiful bodies of intricate design
all touch the living walls
all coast with us on the ocean
all rhyme their own melodies
to chime with ours
silver peals

a song of our land

ab so lute beauty

Biology

Off Azalea
That's where it is
Not so far as Spirit Rock
But close to me is love

Smooth stones
Loamy earth
Branched white tree birch bark
Forked limbs for us to stand in

Moss to lie on
Beds of earthen comfort
Lush body hold close
Lisa watches with camera

Camera watches beatific smiles
In dappled shade
Warm steady breath
Like canyon winds

When the "inept" dancer dances. That is alchemy.
As the sun sets near our horizon, it turns red.
To speak a 'difficult' thought can bring freedom.
To understand our human experience is such a struggle
To communicate…a challenge.
Love is alchemy. Hardships bring change.
I reach for straws

To Jump Out Of The Window

Done in.
Closed over.
Roll me in that bed, alright:
The rug pulled out from under.

Were you not going to be a rock?
Were you not going to be my smooth road, my sandy
beach, my home coming at last?
Were you not going to be there to catch me when I fall?
Were you not that dream that makes pavement out of
candy floss?

Did I think there was no bitter price to pay, my sweet?
Did I think that the past would not mark the future?
Did I think that tar would not seep, would not crack,
would not blister?
Did I think that I was that you were that the sky and
the earth and the balance of it all

The balance of it all
the stones tumble
rumble the earthquake's wave
and the candy dish breaks
and the chocolate egg bursts
and the vase spills
and we get to mop up
and get to crouch on the earth
and our heads touch on the floor
and we giggle
and roll over

WILL
YOU
STILL
LOVE
ME
IF
I
DONT
LET
YOU
EAT
SPAGHETTI
OFF
MY
BELLY
TONIGHT

;-)

Can you   feel   my kiss on your   finger-tip?
Can you   feel my kiss on your   wrist?
Can you   feel my kiss on your   shin?
Can you feel   my   lips on your   collarbone?
Can you   feel my   lips on your   hip?
Can you   feel   my lips   in the nape of your   neck?
Can you feel my   tongue beneath your   ear?
Can you feel   my tongue   deep down
on your   back?
Can you   feel   my tongue drawing a
word   on   yours?
Can you feel us?   We speak.

Mysteries of the universe
deep knowledge.
the cosmic egg

Life on other planets
Space travel
Time warps
Windows in time
Time travel.

I ve never been to mars
Never been to jupiter
Never been to venus
Or titan the big methane rivered moon of Saturn

But I do travel with you
And I do experience much of what, to science,
is invisible.
Love made visible in electrical storms inside your female
body
Eruptions of atoms and molecules all working
in tandem
Thought and wired brain mind body and soul
all communicating at once

Soft flesh so alive
You so far away do answer the radio telescopes call that
extends from light years afar

I go to mars
I go to jupiter

I go to venus
The methane rivers of titan
You are the life
The cosmic egg
The secret unraveled

I go there
And you come to me
And its all so obvious why we exist at all.

Zydeco rhythm in the swamp
rolls me in the reeds
rolls me in the heron's nest
in the tall tall grass
my hand on my ankle
my thigh against my breast
my hair grows wild and long
twists into the folds of my form
I kick my heel
beat the ground
open the wings
of my collarbone
of my pelvis
of the small bones in my toes
and emerge
wet inside my ears
as the shards fall away
bright violet in the evening light
dappled, patterns familiar
a map of my time
a map of a beach I cannot remember
a map of a water course that bore me
shards crumple beneath the sole of my foot
stance shift dance step release moist earth
stone shift weed blade cling yellow petal
there, in that moment, the smell of the nectar and
I come to the sea

At the Gynecologist's

There are qualities in the material world that are seldom experienced; only necessity makes them apparent...d drake

Who are we but Atoms
Partly visible. Partly invisible.
Particles of love
Radiating poetry. Art. Philosophy.
I see myself through you and around you
As the world turns
You hold me in and about you
My curves fold on you
We meet turning into
We touch
Our Matter

You might not want children because
issues in his family
gene dance
she said, our chirpy gynecologist,
looking straight at me, slant at my lover
instruments out

What can be seen
What can be talked about
What is love
What is form
What is dance

Love him, but not children like him?
White coat atoms settle into their dance:
dream plane, wish bone, Galton's galvanized knowledge
eugenic technology that flies off our bodies' awkward
edges
erasure of the spastic tender
touch, deliberate, the vaginal membrane

> The air in this place is heavy...like water
> We glide and float
> outer space
> For our otter bodies
> Playground
> You and I twirl in this ether of darkness and light.

The gynecologist motions him to come closer,
to look upon the universe
cervix's eye into the inner coil
behold this scene
biological biopsy punches its hole into
the donut of infinity:
Schroedinger's cat is alive inside me
black box theatre
cage

I do, in part, rely on the kindness of strangers
Often it hurts me for people to be generous
I need to be clear on what care is.
You go first.
No. after you.
Crash. An accident.
Wasn't that how the bomb was discovered...by accident ?

we go to the hot springs
and are greeted at the entry gate by an older man with
scruffy hair and long beard
he tells us we are the adventurous sort
because we travel with two wheelchairs and no 'helper'
he says his name is Basil, which means kingly.
He says I remind him of steven hawkings
Whom he admires tremendously.
I look away and roll my eyes.
I forgive him anyway.
The king and I.
Hot springs all over the world are connected volcanically.

Petra asks the nurse in the drs office how it is to be
working on Christmas eve.
Its awful. I hate you she says.

                                          I hate you

Just kidding she says. Im really ok.
No matter

                                          No matter

How am I ?
One of the hardest questions I answer.
Alchemy. Alchemic ?
Dancing between thought and movement.
On the edges of present and eternity.
A socialist.
A poet. A dreamer.
Lost in space and time.
Not quite knowing how I am.
Feeling
Where do I come from ?
Arachnid brain stem of evolution.
Fills in the gap

```
             curled
          asleep   around
     fall                your
     I         love        curl
          spiral           in
          gnarled  nautilus
                 shell
```

Two: Cripple Poetics

The Question of Cripple
The Metaphor of Wind in Cripple Poetics
By Neil Marcus

How can I speak of cripple and not mention the wind.
How can I speak of crippled and not mention the heart.
Heart, wind, song, flower, space, time, love. To leave
these absent is to leave cripple in stark terms.
As if we were made of medical parts and not flesh and
bone.

There is always wind in my cripple
Off shore breezes.
Scented nightflowering vines.
Wild salsa dances that run past midnight

Cripple is not extraordinary or ordinary.
Cripple is a full plate
A blown about newspaper
An ox in a rice field, ploughing earth

Petra writes: I love this poem, and what you tease out of
this word that so many crip culture poets are fascinated
by: 'cripple' is so much richer than 'disabled' as a sound,
as an image, bound to a longer heritage. Rippling wind
waves on oceans, earth furrows, the zen movement of
sand and rice patterns, a chair's mark on the ground: the
sensuality of the word and your world merge as I mouth
the words. Rejected trash becomes an object of beauty,
moving in its own gravity. You told me that you wrote this
poem in response to one of mine that you liked, Crip
Language, a poem I wrote a while back. In it, cripple has a
very different, harsher vocabulary.

Neil writes: yes, it is clear in your poem below that the word cripple is not a "hip" word. It is ancient and is born of cruelty and violence. there is no illusion that it is "cool". That's the reality, lest we forget. you remind us of it here. There is another reality that needs expression that comes from our resistance to the stereotype and its pain. It s a delicate balance. Both sides needing acknowledgement; the wind and the kruppel/gruppen.

Crip Language
By Petra Kuppers

Krüppel Cripple Fickle Tickle
playground ground go round again
last out on the line
Cripple Fucking Krüppel Mädchen
tickle fickle root
Krücke Crutch Crotch kicked away
blow me one, here, gut
fuck off
fick Dich Selbst
Cripple Ripple Cripple Ripple
stick that stick across your feet
fall on down
fall on down
that stick is harder than your bone

Petra writes: we find what we need in the words we call our own: anger and tenderness, affirmation and defense. The crip and its painful history: in my poem, I remember sexual violence, and the use of the word 'crip' in gang contexts. I find it deeply satisfying to read my poem out loud, to use its rhythms like a shield, like a ritual, but the

poem also holds for me memories of isolation. My two languages come together and clash, rhyme and diverge. I claim
space with my breath.

Neil writes: I don't use the word crip to describe myself.
I don't wish to take on its painful history. I love the way you
face the utter darkness and despair surrounding our history.
You name it then I feel we are all free to move on. "that
stick" that once was so punishing comes creatively alive in a
new narrative…
To put "wind" in "crip"

Petra writes: Crip and cripple, as words in disability culture
poetics: we have talked about this often, via email, exploring
the term 'crips' and how we each feel about the term.

Neil writes:

when you call us crips
I cant see or feel your 'wink'
when you refer to me as a vegetable

or im vegetative
i feel more at ease

is there any humor in crip

maybe wry crips

is our history similarly known to ourselves or the public
as african americans is known

not yet

then why do we borrow a nigger equivalent—is it?—use
of oppressive term for ownership of power

this is my poorly developed opening discussion
even tho im nitwit –not without wit–

neil ;-)

And Petra replies:

As always, you catch me off-step: do I reply to this as a
poem, refer to the way it dances across the screen, or as
an argument, a statement in a different form? Both, of
course, but the dual shape captures me.

In terms of word sound, I personally do not like crip - I like
cripple, rippling across my tongue, little explosions, waves
in my mouth. Liquid, and reminding me of Krüppel, my
German word, that from early on in the German movement was used as a word of coming together, in Krüppel
Gruppen (cripple groups). Krüppel is also a German word
for stick: something to beat with. There's an anger in the
word, and its echoes. I am not sure the English crip has
the same richness there, at least not for me: it's too short,
too hip.

But you rightly point to wry crips: as soon as there's a history to a word, a chain of associations, we can love it?

But is there not humor in 'crip'? I like it because it has
multi-national meaning: an Australian comic artist uses
the label, people all over the globe use it, and there's an
upbeatness in it, the 'crip, crip, crip', like an insistent
melody.

It is a counterword, a reclamation of the master's language, I agree, and holds the violences of the master (world) firmly in its sound. Is that a bad thing? I am not sure...

I like your reference to the unknown nature of our history, and how, therefore, it is harder to have the oppositional tones in the word. Good point: but then, if we do not use a provisional word that speaks harder than 'disabled people,' how will we ever open up the silences in our history?

Provisional word: that seems to me important in any discussion of 'crip.' It will serve us, for a while, as so many people are only slowly coming to a political and artistic understanding of what it means to lead a rich disabled life.

Neil answers:

i learned recently that i dont like it said of me
that i have dystonia
however to say i am dystonic
is ok
i feel too that i am not a crip
thats not who i am
i like this word Kruppelgruppen
perhaps creeper too
behindenmensch,no
shapeshifter,yes
trickster ok
artist ok
mortal YES
foil of the goddess and god realm
neural collective on earth

Petra writes:

Storms and breezes, wind and blows – I note that your last word is 'earth', which brings me back to your opening poem, and the ploughed earth. We have to labor to earn our words, to make our world. Poetry allows us to explore cripple life in its many nuances, and we can hold up different angles of our languages' crystals. Through the prisms of our languages, our experiences, our senses, we can see a cripple poetics.

Three: Echoes

Kuppers and Marcus

Disabled Country

by Neil Marcus

If there was a country called disabled,
I would be from there.
I live disabled culture, eat disabled food,
make disabled love, cry disabled tears,
climb disabled mountains and tell disabled stories.
If there was a country called disabled,
I would say she has immigrants that come to her
from as far back as time remembers.
If there was a country called disabled,
then I am one of its citizens.
I came there at age 8. I tried to leave.
Was encouraged by doctors to leave.
I tried to surgically remove myself from disabled country
but found myself, in the end, staying and living there.
If there was a country called disabled,
I would always have to remind myself that I came from
there.
I often want to forget.
I would have to remember…to remember.
In my life's journey
I am making myself
at home in my country.

Crip Music

by Petra Kuppers

A beat behind, sycophant, you
Sisyphus, roll and run
again and again
Sybil whistle tune, mournfully
whistle in the dark
the shoe steps the rhythm
behind, behind, behind you
with the crutch cane stick beat
the cripple who ripples across
the street with the wheel on the rack
rackle and giggle the cripple
till the music stops
we step out
and then, and then, it builds
the sound, and the beat
and the melody of the cane
and the melody of the crutch
and the melody of the wheel
and the tap of the stick
and the tick of ventilators
dilate, pulse
push breath through the street
roll forward and on
the beat in a circle
we move, we move
the line held firm
the song lifting

About Petra Kuppers

Petra Kuppers grew up in Germany, left when she was twenty-four, moved to Wales for ten years and learned about the disability culture movement, moved to the US East Coast, then to New Zealand, and back to the US, first to Texas, then to Michigan. Now she shuttles between Ann Arbor and Berkeley. She is a disability culture activist, a community artist, Artistic Director of The Olimpias Performance Research Projects, and an Associate Professor of English, Theatre and Dance, and Women's Studies at the University of Michigan. Her books include *Disability and Contemporary Performance: Bodies on Edge* (Routledge, 2003), *The Scar of Visibility: Medical Performances and Contemporary Art* (Minnesota, 2007) and *Community Performance: An Introduction* (Routledge, 2007). She likes to move, and was one of the first wheelchair users to gain a professional dance qualification. These days, she code-switches from tri-pedal cane walking to manual chair wheeling to scooter movement to electric wheelchair walk. She rather writes poems than revealing biographical statements.

About Neil Marcus

Neil Marcus...Born in the snowy suburbs of New York City, grew up in Ojai, CA, lives in Berkeley, CA. TV and film actor.poet.writer.butoh dancer.contact improvisational lover. Lecturer with a twist.

My main education comes from acquiring Dystonia at age 8.and I was much influenced by the human growth movement in the 60s and 70s.

I began acting seriously after writing and performing in the autobiographical play STORM READING which ended up touring from 1988-1998. I performed it over 300 times.

I have worked with this key idea: disability is not a brave struggle or courage in the face of adversity, disability is an art.

In an oral history interview for a national collection of artists with disabilities, I used the technology of instant messaging to articulate this:

Neil Marcus66<!-- (11:00:58 AM)-->: im a human bridge in a moment of time spanning as far and as relevant as my thoughts will carry me

About Lisa Steichmann

Lisa Steichmann is a photographer and book artist in Ann Arbor, Michigan. She teaches at Washtenaw Community College, and is a collaborator of The Olimpias. Her work has been shown nationally, including regionally at Detroit Artist's Market and C-Pop, Detroit; Kettle Pond Visitor Center, Rhode Island, and the Slusser Gallery at the University of Michigan. Lisa's work explores the flow of motion captured in the stillness of the image. She investigates the relationships between people, their movement, and the environment in the photographic moment. She is delighted to work with Neil and Petra, their joy in each other and the friendship in the circle, the laughter, the hugs. Her photos capture this human touch and the depth of friendship. From April through October, Lisa and Petra can most often be found swimming or kayaking together in the lakes and streams nearby.

About Homofactus Press

The mission of Homofactus Press is to publish books that discuss our complicated relationships to our bodies and identities, with all the complexities and contraditions such an endeavor entails. To learn more about us, please visit http://www.homofactuspress.com

Breinigsville, PA USA
11 March 2010
234051BV00001B/45/P